The Descent Of Bolshevism

Ameen Fares Rihani

THE
DESCENT OF
BOLSHEVISM

BY
AMEEN RIHANI

Author of
The Book of Khalid, etc.

BOSTON
THE STRATFORD CO., Publishers
1920

Copyright 1920
The STRATFORD CO., Publishers
Boston, Mass.

The Alpine Press, Boston, Mass., U. S. A.

TO MY FRIEND

MICHAEL MONAHAN

AN ESSAYIST OF RARE CHARM, A PHILOSOPHER
OF BROAD HUMAN SYMPATHIES, AN
APOSTLE OF FREEDOM AND SANITY
IN LITERATURE AND LIFE

THIS LITTLE BOOK IS DEDICATED

CONTENTS

v

SEEDS FOR THE SOWER

Russia cries, Proletariat! History echoes, Sans-culotte.

The rule of the Proletariat is another swing of the pendulum of Time.

Autocracy is a government of the few from above; Bolshevism is a government of the few from below.

Society may be likened to a rod, which only a just government can balance properly. But we are still trying to find the balancing point.

Bolshevism is the other end of Czarism.

In a true democracy is the cure for most of our social and political ills; but a few of them must remain to keep us going.

A true democratic government is still an ideal to be attained.

vii

Revolution is glorified by intellectuals, apotheosized by poets, sanctified by visionaries, and bled white by politicians.

Revolution applies a local anaesthetic to one class of Society and operates on the other.

Bolshevism may be Marxian in theory, but it is Hulagoesque in practice. It may be of European descent, but it is Oriental in tradition, Oriental in mood, Oriental in temperament.

The Orientals are the extremists of the world. As individuals, they are slaves of Caprice; as types, they are slaves of Authority. The one knows no law, the other knows no exception to the law.

The Oriental in the Russian has set the House of Socialism on fire; and the European in the Russian has not yet found the fire extinguisher.

Foreword

More than once in history have people revolted against the inequalities of life and refused to submit to the restraints of laws and creeds. They have often gone through a period of communism and red terror in the hope of realizing ultimately the Perfect State. Their leaders, undoubtedly sincere at first, espouse the utopian dream, declaring themselves the exponents of its ideals, the promised messengers of its blessings. But with the material for revolt ready at hand, and unable to resist the seductions of nascent power, they soon undergo that transformation which history identifies, often not unjustly, with demagogy, if they fail, or with autocracy, if they succeed.

In either case, by utilizing the elements of negation in Society, they become apos-

tles of violence, proclaiming the theory of
"creative destruction." But instead of
creating a utopia on the ruins of their
making, they only succeed in setting up, as
history shows, another government, which,
no matter how just and sound its founda-
tions are in theory, soon becomes in practice more despotic and corrupt.

But the vision of the Perfect State,
which awakens a people from the stupor
of slavery, arouses them to revolt, fires
them with dazzling promises, and leads
them to self-sacrifice, to martyrdom, to destruction, continues, nevertheless, to leaven
the aspirations of succeeding nations. The
theory of "eternal recurrence" is insepa-
rable, it seems, from the theory of "creative destruction."

And no matter how ambitious and sincere, or how selfish and unscrupulous are
the leaders of the movements that embody
this theory, no matter how ruthless and
uncompromising are the apostles of equality and violence, the nation they overturn
soon or late finds its balance again and,

FOREWORD

through the agencies of law and order, re-
establishes on a higher plane the principles
of justice and progress.

For, as a rule, a nation emerges stronger,
morally and spiritually, from a revolution-
ary upheaval. With this single exception,
however, all the movements of the world
that sought to establish, by the dagger,
the sword, the bayonet, the machine gun,
or even by peaceful communities, a utopia
on earth, have been doomed to failure.

The extremists, no matter how long and
brilliant their temporary success, have
gone the way of all political despots and
all religious impostors. And their culpa-
bility is not in plunging a nation into
anarchy and crime, but in debasing the
ideals of utopia, by yoking them with
the destructive agencies of negation in a
people.

This is true of the ancient as well as the
modern world, as I shall endeavor to show
in these chapters, tracing the more prominent movements in history against the
existing order of things. The only differ-

ence is in the background and the surroundings, which give the movements distinct local colors and strange sounding names.

As a rule, however, the tyranny of inequality has been at the bottom of all revolts and revolutions. Only that in the past it was embodied in religions and autocracies, today it is embodied in industrialism. The masters in the past were the kings and priests, while in our times they are the captains of industry and the labor leaders. Under either condition, however, a long-suffering and downtrodden people will be driven ultimately to extremes of materialism expressed in universal negations.

CHAPTER I
Mazdak and Mazdakism

This is the Bolshevism we meet with, as early as the fifth century, in Persia. Its exponent and leader, a man named Mazdak, was a priest in Neishapur before he became a prophet. King Kobad, the little father of the great Nushirvan, was then on the throne; and Christianity, which had penetrated Persia, was still convulsed by the controversies of the single and the double nature of Christ and the persecutions that generally followed or accompanied them.

The theology of the Fathers and the philosophy of St. Paul carried the dissensions through Armenia to Persia, thus weakening the newly acquired faith, which had but a slight hold upon the people. It certainly had little or no influence upon King Kobad. As for Mazdak, he must have found his original inspiration in St. Paul. "The law worketh wrath; where no law is, there is no transgression." This he announced as a divine revelation to the people and proceeded to draw his own conclusions and enlarge upon them. His second revelation was that all men are born equal and have a right to maintain this equality through life. His third: Everything belongs to God, and it is impious in man to claim or to appropriate to himself what is the property of the Creator.

The law worketh wrath; all men are born equal; God is the direct source and owner of all things: with these three cardinal doctrines, Mazdak embarked upon his utopian career, pursuing the fatal phantom of his logic. He took St. Paul by the letter, shaking the spirit out of his words. Or he may not have been endowed with sufficient grace to see the true essence of the Gospel, considering as mere theology or mysticism such doctrines as are calculated to elevate the believer to the free life of the spirit.

[2]

THE DESCENT OF BOLSHEVISM

Mazdak wanted freedom—the sort of freedom, in fact, that is today the object of popular clamor. "Where no law is, there is no transgression." St. Paul was twisted into a universal negation, which Mazdak pretended to have discovered, through the medium of Fire, in Zoroaster's own divine bosom. For he would destroy the new religion by invoking the aid of the old. And he would establish the reign of perfect equality on earth to justify divine ownership and power. For if all titles of worldly things are vested in God, they are destined for the common use of all human kind.

Mazdak's three cardinal fallacies were more attractive, indeed, to the people than Christianity. And they were excellent vehicles for a counter-movement. Mazdak moved and many others moved with him. In spite of his initial success, however, he knew that, without royal sanction and support, the new Temple—the Temple of Fire and Freedom and Common Ownership— would not long endure. But with a king and a prophet at its head, the new cult would spread, would prosper, would triumph. The prophet was there; and he set out to convert the king. His qualifications were traditional. He began by setting the first example in sanctity and abstemiousness. He clothed himself in coarse wool, denied himself at first all worldly things, and retired into seclusion for meditation and prayer.

And when King Kobad demanded a miracle before he embraced the new faith, he was not disappointed. Mazdak invited him to the Temple, where he heard the Fire speaking to the Prophet. The fact that a man was hidden behind the altar to lend the flames a tongue, did not much matter. From Tabari to Gibbon, all historians agree that Mazdak was a downright impostor. They are also agreed that Kobad was a royal scoundrel. The new cult appealed to him for more than one reason, and he was predisposed to accept any penny wonder as divine.

For he had an illicit carnal desire which

[4]

could be sanctioned only by some such religion as Mazdakism. "He was not nice in point of conscience," as one historian puts it; nor was he happy on the throne. His brother and his courtiers cast an enchantment upon his crown and, as soon as he became a Mazdakite, they whisked it away. And he was cast into prison as a warning to Mazdak and his followers. But the warning was of no avail; for in addition to a prophet and a king, the movement gained the support of a queen. Kobad's wife became an ardent Mazdakite. And by smiling assent to the jailer one night, she succeeded in having her husband, hidden in a mattress, carried away. This was a signal triumph for the new cult. And Mazdak, son of Bambadan, thereafter called himself the Sign, the Demonstration, the Word, the Redeemer.

And his followers set out zealously, violently to prove themselves faithful to his creed. Everything was to be held in common, "Goods, Women, Children and the Rest." And for more than fifty years

[5]

there was no relaxation in the practice, which, of course, was accompanied by plunder and bloodshed, by all the crimes, in fact, that lawlessness and anarchy engender. Everywhere his votaries seized the wives, the daughters and the property of others. And the King could not punish them, having become himself a Mazdakite.

When Kobad escaped from prison, he fled to the White Huns, a powerful tribe of Central Asia, who invaded Persia, and were defeated by the great Bahram Gur, to whom Omar pays the mocking tribute:

"And Bahram, the Great Hunter, the wild Ass
Stamps o'er his Head, but can not break
his sleep."

But the White Huns were still camping on the frontier, awaiting the opportunity for another Great Offensive. The opportunity came when Kobad arrived and straightway made an alliance with his country's enemies. And at the head of an army of White Huns he led the invasion, entered the capital in triumph, smote his infidel brother off the throne and regained the crown.

And Mazdakism, which had suffered a momentary check in his absence, became again a power of terror and frightfulness in the land. In the name of Equality, Lawlessness and Communism, the tables were turned, every crime was sanctioned or condoned, the rich, in consequence, becoming poor, the poor becoming rich, and everywhere the mob ruled supreme. Morality and religion were renounced, abolished; man became a law unto himself; and the strong, whether of the proletariat or the bourgoisie of those times, prevailed.

But the most amazing things about Mazdakism, is the inconsistency that is scarcely found outside the Orient, where piety and crime go hand in hand. For while it encouraged, even sanctioned all kinds of unspeakable abominations, it imposed upon its followers a rigid observance of the sacredness of animal life. Mazdak himself was a vegetarian, and he prohibited the killing of animals for food or for sport.

[7]

Indeed, to kill a man who had an abundance of the things of the world, was in his eye, a virtue; but to kill even an insect was a crime. And he continued to pray and to wear coarse wool even in his last days, when his own wealth and his harim were re-distributed among the people. How true of him the Arabic couplet:

"He wore bells on his sandals to warn
the insects from his path,
While in his hand the dripping dagger
sought the victims of his wrath."

When King Kobad died, his son the Great Nushirvan took a real pious interest in the new cult. He introduced it to the higher equality, led it to the final communism—Death. On his coronation he made a speech worthy of a great monarch, in which he promised many good things to all his subjects and called upon them to help him make good his promise. Whereupon, he ordered the chiefs of the Sect, Tabari, tells us to appear before him and had their heads cut off. Others say that he imitated Jehu in the Book of Kings. Which means that he had the Mazdakites assemble in the Temple, and at his command, his executioners descended upon them and introduced them in a jiffy to the higher equality.

And he issued an edict abolishing the practice of Mazdakism and confirming the domestic rights of Society. The wealth and property of the Mazdakites were divided among the poor; such as could be identified were returned to their lawful owners; and the women held in the slavery of communism were freed and given the option of either returning to their former homes or of remaining, as legal wives, with whom they had accustomed themselves to live.

Such was the justice of Nushirvan. But in spite of the heads that were cut off and the Jehu method of extermination, Mazdakism continued to squirm in the dust and succeeded in making its way to other lands. For the new law of the community of women was later observed and promul-

gated in Syria; and, with the other doctrines of Mazdak, it spread to the West
and was embraced, archeologists tell us,
by what remained of the ancient Gnostics.

CHAPTER II
The Khawarij

In Arabia, after the death of Mohammed, a party of extremists and fanatics renounced all existing authority, civil and religious, proclaiming Allah their only Master and Sovereign. The Prophet himself is more or less responsible for their action; for having given the Arabs a religion, a form of constitution, and a moral code, he failed to lay down or suggest any rule governing the right of succession. The field was open to any of his friends and companions who had the will, the power and the ill fortune to succeed him. The first two, however, commanded the confidence and obtained the suffrage of the Faithful. The third was the first to be assassinated; and the fourth, Ali, who ultimately met with the same fate as his predecessor, had many rival candidates, among them the powerful and wily Moawia. Forty years after the Prophet's death, therefore, the state of Islam was shaken by wars and torn by tribal strife.

This was not promising, was not edifying. And among the people who revolted against one claimant or another, were the group of extremists I have mentioned, who renounced them all and would obey only the Koran. The Prophet, they argued, did not name a successor, laid down no rule for the succession, did not evidently believe in delegating his divine power to man. The three leaders, Ali, Moawia and Amru, are all usurpers and it is the right of true Muslem to deny them their suffrage. Nay, it is their pious duty, in order to uphold Islam, to get rid of them all.

The Khawarij, or Seceders who started this movement, were the only so-called orthodox Muslems who, reading between the lines of the Holy Book, were able to con the esoteric wisdom and the divine will. All power emanates from God—a variation of Mazdak's *All titles are vested in*

[12]

God—and mankind is responsible to Him alone. He is the one and only ruler, and they the Khawarij would recognize no other. Those that claimed to be vicars of God and his Prophet on earth, are usurpers, therefore, and impostors. Islam should not be ruled by an autocrat called khalif or imam, but by local councils elected by the people. This is the democracy that was so dear to the Arabs even before the Prophet; and the Khawarij called themselves the only true apostles of Mohammedanism and democracy. And they would proclaim its reign by the sword; they would reduce its enemies by assassination.

Accordingly, three of their leaders met one day in the Kaaba and swore by the Black Stone and the Koran to carry out their criminal plan. Each one of the conspirators chose his victim; and Ali, Moawia and Amru were to be assassinated at one appointed day and hour. But the plot was discovered and the Khawarij decided to fight in the open like true Arabs. They declared war on Ali and his rivals in the field; but they were defeated by Ali's forces in the battle of Nahrawan. They were dispersed; they were not crushed. Instead of a united army, they broke up into various sects, who conducted a secret propaganda both in Arabia and Persia against the civil and spiritual authority of Islam. The Prophet is dead, but Allah liveth forever. This was the slogan that was whispered in secret councils and was yet to shake the very foundation of the Faith.

It was not heard of, after the defeat of the Khawarij, for over a hundred years. But in the ninth century, Abdallah ibn Maimoun Kaddah of Ahwaz revived it and expanded upon it. He was wise enough to see, however, that not until his followers were strongly united and well armed would the method of the Khawarij be favorable to him and his ideals. For he was a man of lofty ideals, this Persian of Ahwaz. He began by founding a secret society which was to bind together Arabs and Persians,

Muslems, Christians and Jews,—indeed,
all mankind. Kaddah had political ambition also, which he could not realize by
openly antagonizing the existing governments. But he proclaimed a new right of
succession.

There was Ismail, the son of the sixth
Imam after Ali and descendant from Ali's
line. And Kaddah, who was a master of
mystic lore, ingeniously evolved the theory of hidden and revealed successors to
the Prophet. Ismail, he claimed, was the
last revealed, and since his death the succession continued through hidden or un-
incarnate imams. But he, Kaddah, awaiting the psychological moment, harbored
the secret purpose, the ambition of proclaiming himself to Islam the first revealed imam and khalif after Ismail. He
died, however, a disappointed man. For
one named Obeidullah was the founder of
the new dynasty. But Kaddah and his followers were nevertheless called Ismailites,
a name that even today is despised and

dreaded by orthodox Mohammedans, because to them it is synonymous with infidelity, immorality, anarchy and crime.

For Kaddah's secret society was founded on a universal negation and wrapt in a crazy-quilt of philosophy. Its deep mysteries were revealed only to those who had attained the highest degree of the Order. It had novices and missionaries called *dais* to preach its political and outwardly religious doctrines. It offered inducements to all classes and creeds and led them on, from a mystical interpretation of Islam— the Ismailite method was allegorical—to a total renunciation of its teachings. ''The inner doctrine,'' says one Orientalist, ''was philosophical and eclectic.'' In other words, Mazdakism was resuscitated; the Khawarij idea was taken down from the shelf and dusted; and both were invested with the dignity of Neo-Platonic and Neo-Pythagorian wisdom. But in their interpretation of the Koran, some of the Ismailite doctors pushed the allegory so far that it ended in nothing less than the aboli-

tion of all public worship and the foundation of a purely philosophic—in name—
and a very licentious moràl code—in re-
ality—on the ruins of all revelations and
all civil and spiritual authority.

CHAPTER III

The Karmathians

Among the foremost disciples of Kaddah of Ahwaz was an Arab of Bahrein called Karmat or Quermut, who in the latter part of the ninth century (880 A. D.) established in Irak a secret society of his own and, like his master Kaddah, took to preaching in allegories. Like him too, he taught the doctrine of "hidden and revealed imams," but he added that while the imam is hidden, his cause must be revealed and upheld by missionaries. And he, Hamdan Quermut, first assumed this modest role and soon became the leader of a new movement. It is curious how his followers were transformed by degrees, as they advanced in the secret order, from true and pious Mohammedans to atheists and anarchists, in a word, to Mazdakites.

His ladder, which was broad at the base,

tapered at the top to a point, from which the Karmathian plunged headlong into a regenerated world of absolute freedom and equality. The Koran is full of mysteries, Quermut warned the climber as he set his ladder firmly on the ground of faith; and mysteries must be taught and explained. The early teachers of Islam were often wrong; only seven imams are infallible; the others are all in error. Climb, climb higher. Every infallible imam had a prophet who was obeyed in all things; the last imam was Ismail. Another step, and Quermut is his prophet. Still another, and the traditions vanish from view. The next disposes of religion itself; prayers, fasting, alms, the pilgrimage are no longer essential to salvation. For behold, you are reaching the top, the vanishing point and you are free to entertain any belief or unbelief so long as you recognize no authority, temporal or spiritual, but that of Quermut, the new Prophet. Thus the Karmathian gradually sheds his creed, renounces his faith, but is in duty bound

to fight against all Muslem power and
authority.

For since Islam combined the spiritual
and civil power in one ruler called khalif
and imam, these secret societies were orig-
ginally a protest against one or more of its
tenets as well as against its established
governments. And since it was founded
as much on the sword as on the Koran, and
united in the person of the khalif the func-
tions of pontiff and sovereign, almost in
all the sects, secret or otherwise, the chief
ground of the schism is the contested succession to the throne. And the Karmathians, who secretly coveted the throne,
made certain concessions at first to religion. But while they adopted the two
fundamental doctrines of Islam, that is,
the omnipotence of God and the fixedness
of Fate, they declared all the others, even
as the Wahhabys of today, vain and futile.
Nay, they are snares contrived to exalt a
certain portion of mankind at the expense
of the vast majority. And they the Karmathians would free the majority from

these snares. They would utterly destroy
the foundation of all existing order, set
men free from the despotism of all morals
and laws and creeds, and re-establish their
direct allegiance to God.

Some of these so-called high mysteries
are entertained also by the Sufis of today.
But Sufism does not prompt to action and
rebellion. The Sufi detaches himself from
the world and all its tyrannies and evils,—
rises on the ladder to the vanishing point,
so to speak, and stays there, — while the
Karmathians, the Ismailites and other kin-
dred sects, would fight to substitute the
reign of Allah for the reign of man on
earth. And the Arab is no where so well
at home as in metaphysical abstractions
and the desert. He is most credulous, is
more believing, in fact, than religious. His
deep sense of the possibilities that may be
hidden in the depths of the unknown, in-
duces in him a ready easy credence in any
message supposedly divine. If one prophet,
why not another? Mohammed has by no
means closed the Arab nation's account

with Allah. This is the religious reason for Quermut's great success. The political reason is still more plausible.

The Abbaside khalifs were usurpers. Most of them were tyrants and profligates. Moreover, they favored the foreigners at court, even though they secretly plotted against them, more than they did the Arabs. The Khalif Mo'tasem's Turkish guards at the palace soon became a power in Baghdad. And the Karmathians, aroused by their intrigues, found in them additional cause for revolt. They disclaimed the Abbasides, abhorred their worldly pomp, denounced their tyranny and their unpatriotic conduct, and finally declared war upon them. Their battle-cry was, "Allah liveth forever, Allah sufficeth us!"

And combining thus the religious and the political issues, based on the wholesale negations excepting only Allah, for both worlds, they raised the standard of revolt; and for a century or more they were a terror to the Khalifs of Baghdad and the undisputed masters of Arabia.

And Quermut, not long after his first missionary activities, became the Prophet, the Guide, the Director. He was also called the Camel, the Word, even the Holy Ghost—the Herald of the Messiah. The Millenium madness, which was upon Europe at that time, had reached, it seems, Arabia, and Quermut, the Universal, incorporated it into his Scheme of Salvation.

Most of his followers were of the Beduin tribes, who found Islam too irksome, too exacting, and were ready to join any movement that would offer encouragement to their liberal and looting spirit. And they were desperate, indomitable fighters. Under the leadership of two Generals, Abu-Said and his son Abu Taher, they conquered first the provinces of Oman and Bahrein and established themselves at Hasa behind the burning sands of the Red Desert, where they themselves were secure against any attack or invasion. Northward they marched to Irak, laying waste everything before them; to upper Syria, where they stormed and captured the city of Baalbek, putting its inhabitants to the sword. There were no novices among the Karmathians in action, at war. They all had mastered the higher mysteries, and were fighting like demons to establish the reign of Allah on earth. No army of the Khalifs could withstand their desperate attacks and their slaughter. They threw themselves into the jaws of death, blindly obeying the command of their leaders.

But Mecca is the ultimate goal of every Muslim, and every Muslim rebellion. Without it, no victory is complete. Towards Mecca, therefore, commanded by Abu Taher, the Karmathians swept over the desert. And like swarms of locusts, wave after wave, they descended upon the City at the height of the pilgrimage season and committed, in the name of Allah, the most unspeakable crimes and abominations. Thirty thousand of the pilgrims were slain; the well of Zamzam was choked with the dead; the House of God, the Kaaba, was polluted; the Holy Veil was torn in shreds; and the Black Stone, the most sacred relic of Islam, was carried off to Hasa. But it was restored twenty years later.

And although their atrocities had the effect of uniting for a time all the Mohammedan factions against them, they continued for many years after the capture of Mecca and the sacking of the Kaaba, to achieve one victory after another and spread the terror of their power in the land. It was a war waged by anarchy and rapine, not only against Islam, but against Society and all organized governments. "The sect of the Karmathians," says Gibbon, "may be considered as the second cause of the decline and fall of the empire of the Khalifs."

And the death of Abu Taher, their great General, may be considered as one of the principal causes of the decline and fall of the Karmathians. The Beduins themselves, who first joined the movement and were chiefly responsible for its success, turned against it when its power began to wane. At the close of the tenth century,

[25]

after the death of Abu Taher, the Karmathians were defeated in Irak and soon
after they lost the control of the pilgrimage. The Beduin tribes therefore had no
longer any use for them. Not only did
they refuse them their support, but they
revolted against what remained of their
authority. The revolt became general, and
one after another of the provinces recov-
ered their independence. One Beduin
sheikh alone, it is stated, besieged and took
Katif, the capital of Bahrein.

The Wahhabys of today continue to rule
in Hasa, maintaining their independence
even against the new King of Hijaz. And
under their Mohammedan puritanism is
the smouldering fire of the Karmathians.
They, too, once captured and sacked the
Holy City of Mecca and still nourish, under
the guise of piety and the assumption of
learning, the most dangerous designs
against it and Islam.

Like the Mazdakites, like the Khawarij,
the Karmathians were not completely destroyed. They had other successors than

the Wahhabys. Straggling bands of free-thinkers and freebooters, followers of Abu Taher and Quermut, continued to rove on the borderland of Society till the middle of the eleventh century, when their famous slogan was beginning to be heard among the hills of Persia and Syria and was soon to be embodied in one of the most fiend-ishly criminal movements against law and order that is recorded in the history of the world.

CHAPTER IV

The Assassins

Three students in Neishapur, swearing eternal friendship to each other, entered one day into a fantastic agreement by which they were to circumvent Fortune. Whoever succeeded first, pledged himself to lend a helping hand to the others. The one was destined to power; the other to fame; and the third, to the universal malediction of mankind. Nizam ul-Mulk, who afterwards became vezier to the Sultan Malek Shah; Omar Khayyam, who refused the proffered favors of his former college friend, preferring the Book of Verse and the Jug of Wine; and Hasan ibn Sabah, who was later known and feared as the Old Man of the Mountain, the founder of the Sect of Assassins, were the three young covenanters of Neishapur.

In his early days Hasan nursed the dream of power; and this agreement, which was made at his suggestion, was an insurance policy, as it were, to his dream. And to be sure, Nizam ul-Mulk made good his promise, and Hasan, unlike Omar, was glad to accept the post he secured him at the court of Malek Shah. But as he was not capable of serving any one else but himself, he no sooner sat on the divan of authority than he began to build him a ladder of the favors of his benefactor and former fellow student. Before he had taken the first step, however, which was to be on the very head of Nizam, he was given a lesson in fidelity and gratitude, and politely escorted to the gate. The lesson was wasted upon him, and Nizam was thereafter marked out as one of his enemies. It was Hasan's boast that, with the aid of two faithful friends, he could have overturned the power of "the Turk and the Peasant," meaning the Sultan and his Vezier. For twenty-two years he nursed his grudge, while laying the foundation of his power. His patience, like his rascality, was inexhaustible.

Having fallen at the court of Malek

Shah, Hasan joined the Ismailites, was initiated into their high mysteries and soon became a *dai*, missionary, of persuasive eloquence and zeal. Meanwhile he was planning for new adventures in foreign lands. The Sultan of Egypt at that time was an Ismailite and consequently a rival to the Khalif of Baghdad. Hasan would set forth to Egypt, therefore, to warm his hands at the fire of the Khalif's favor. His fame as an Ismailite *dai* had preceded him. And when the Khalif Mostanser heard he was coming, he sent a delegation to meet and greet him at the border.

Honors were showered upon Hasan. He was received at court as a man of righteousness and piety; he was invited to speak at the Lodge of Cairo; he was made a member of the Council of Wisdom; he was proclaimed the chief bearer of the torch of truth. But soon his fortunes at the court of Mostanser began to radiate his egregious egotism, fostering the seeds of hate and jealousy all around. And his ladder of intrigue for absolute power which he had built, toppled finally under him, and once more he was politely escorted to the gate. Nay, to the castle, where he was to meditate in solitary confinement on the practical uses of fidelity and gratitude. But the castle, as the story goes, fell like a house of cards without any visible cause whatever, before Hasan reached it. Which was looked upon as a divine sign in his favor and decided the Khalif to banish him from Egypt.

He was placed, therefore, on board of a ship which had to weather many storms before it reached the Syrian coast. The stormy sea gave Hasan an opportunity to perform one of those miracles that mark the beginning of a prophet's career. His fellow travellers, who were not students in meteorology, soon became disciples and followers of the new Mahdi, the commander of the winds and waves. In Damascus and Aleppo he sowed, in passing, the seeds of his secret doctrines, which were later to grow into daggers dripping with blood. And on his return to Persia he entrenched himself with a few faithful followers in the mountain fortress of Alamut. This marked the beginning of his power.

The sect of the Assassins was established principally on the tenets of the Karmathians. The only difference being that, instead of waging open war against his enemies, against society in general, Hasan adopted the policy of secret assassination. This required emissaries who would blindly obey his commands. Like the Karmathian, therefore, his sect was formed of different degrees of membership. Those who stood lowest in the order were the novices, the common people. They had to observe the ordinary tenets of Islam. The *dais* or missionaries were a degree higher than the *rafiks* or companions; and they were both taught to believe in nothing and to scoff at the devotion of the Faithful.

But the most important class of the Order was that of the *fadais* or assassins, who were schooled in self-sacrifice and murder. And at the head of it was *Sheikh ul-Jabal*, the Old Man of the Mountain, Hasan ibn

[32]

Sabah, and chief of the three provinces over which his power soon extended. Hasan never forgot his former college friend and benefactor Nizam ul-Mulk. He was certainly a man of enduring grievances and long-cherished grudges. So the Vezier of Malek Shah and his son were the first victims of the Assassins.

The *fadais* were chosen of the youth of the land. Upon them the Old Man of the Mountain chiefly depended, and to them he looked for the consummation of his scheme of universal happiness. To fire their spirits, therefore, and arouse their self-sacrificing zeal, he contrived for them the most seductive pleasures. The valley of Alamut was walled in and a most brilliant garden was laid in the enclosure—a sample on earth of the Prophet's paradise. In it were streams and fountains of milk and honey, and water and wine; bulbuls and nightingales singing to the rose; gazelles prancing in the scented glades; serving boys with faces like the moon; and jasmine covered kiosks where black-eyed huris languished in voluptuous bliss.

Marco Polo gives us a first hand account of this terrestrial paradise, which was designed for the *fadais* to spur them to their bloody task. Hasan's invention was a great success. A *fadai*, we are told, was first given *hasheesh*—hence the name assassins—was drugged into a trance and taken to the garden, where he awoke to find himself surrounded with all kinds of sensual and voluptuous pleasures. He imagined himself in a dream of paradisal bliss. But it lasted only a few days, when he would be drugged again with *hasheesh* and carried out in the same manner as he was carried in.

This foretaste of Paradise, which he was to enjoy in full and forever by executing the will of his Master Hasan, steeled his heart to the boldest and bloodiest deeds. These young *fadais* made no secret of their calling. They were conspicuous for the red caps and girdles they wore and the terror-spreading daggers they carried.

And their bloody deeds were sometimes done in the open and sometimes in the most mysterious manner. King Sanjar once determined to attack the castle of Alamut. But one morning he found near his bed a dagger stuck in the ground and bearing this message: Sultan Sanjar, beware. Had not thy character been respected, the hand which stuck this dagger in the hard ground could with greater ease have stuck it into thy soft bosom. Whereupon, King Sanjar changed his mind.

There is no doubt that Hasan ibn Sabah was a man of penetrating insight and deep worldly wisdom. And he might have become a power at the court of either Malek Shah or the Khalif Mostanser, had he been decent enough to be thoughtful at least of his benefactors. But the imposing rascal would never have become the supreme ruler of a sect that made a profession of crime and a religion of assassination. Still, he must have died a disappointed man. For the thrones he sought to overturn and the religions he tried to destroy by the doublefaced Monster of atheism and piety, of lawlessness and submission, continued, though rudely shaken during his time, to sway the minds and souls of men. And why? Because of the inconsistency and dishonesty that even an assassin or a chief of assassins, with the insight of Hasan, could well have avoided.

But his weakness was that he followed unquestioning in the path of the Ismailites who taught that lawlessness is good for the ruler, but bad for the subject; that the many are held together by the few through the bridle of the law; that religion is for the common people, knowledge and freedom from all restraints for the elect; and that a secret system of atheism and immorality could work the destruction of those in power. Such demoniacal cynicism never established a dynasty, much less a state of any endurance. Mazdakism was more consistent, if not also more sincere. "God the best ruler sufficeth us: nothing is true, all is allowed," said the chiefs and the initiated of the Assassins.

On the other hand, believing sincerely that morality and religion are the best sureties of a nation, the strongest bulwark of a state, they affected an extraordinary sanctity, wearing the coarsest garments and abstaining, in public at least, from wine and sensuous pleasures. Hasan himself, whatever his motive, rarely ventured outside of his castle in Alamut, where he lived a recluse for thirty-five years. But invisible himself, he saw with a thousand eyes the subtle machinations of princes, the sluggish engines of Oriental politics, the veiled altars of inimical sects and creeds. And he was the lord of a thousand secret daggers.

But in the ranks there was often dissension and murmurs of discontent. The reign of assassination, tempered with readings from the Koran, did not always succeed in veiling the high mysteries from the people, who were kept in the bonds of law and religion, while the chiefs often enjoyed every immunity. The disparity was becoming fatal to the cause. And Hasan himself

seems to have had his remorseful moments.
Once, at least, he feared lest he should die
without obtaining a knowledge of the truth!
As a rule, however, his self-confidence and
self-sufficiency triumphed in the end, even
though he recognized the virtue of com-
promise. For on certain occasions, to mol-
lify his followers, he would announce from
the pulpit that the gates of mercy and
grace are open to those who obey him; that
they are the elect of mankind, free from
all the obligations of the law, released from
the burden and bondage of all commands
and prohibitions. Except, of course, his
own. For he, Hasan ibn Sabah, has brought
to them the day of resurrection. A satur-
nalia such as that of the Mazdakites generally followed these pronouncements.

But the dynasties he had set out to des-
stroy,—the Fatemite of Egypt, the Abbaside of Baghdad, the Seljuk of Persia,—
were still standing and holding their
own despite his thousand secret daggers.
Hasan, therefore, would set up one of his
own. And by bribing his followers with

immunity from all laws and his assassins with a foretaste of Paradise, he succeeded in founding the dynasty that spread its red terror in many lands for more than two centuries. He invoked in his aid the Ismailite doctrine of hidden and revealed imams only to strike out one of its main supports. There was to be no more concealed imams; the last of them died before Hasan. Thenceforth, in his political scheme, the imam had to appear or lose his throne by default.

Every one of his successors, therefore, had it proclaimed that he was the promised imam, promised by his predecessor or by Hasan himself. And to preserve and strengthen the new dynasty, each one was to remove certain prohibitions, or rather to extend the immunity from laws and creeds to a greater number of his subjects. One of the rulers won so many adherents because he drank wine openly and freely and indulged in other forbidden practices. They saw in these lawless habits a clear sign of the coming imam who was to do away with all prohibitions. And there was always, to be sure, a coming imam. This was the ideal the people continued to cherish,—the ideal that the leaders forever dandled before their eyes. And as a rule of succession, although marked with poison and slaughter,—the most natural thing in the world,—it was an improvement upon all the others.

But the inconsistencies of these Old Men of the Mountain sometimes reach the sublime. We have no reason to doubt that Hasan himself, unlike Mazdak four centuries before him, lived the life of an ascetic in his castle on the hilltop. The miniature paradise, which he could behold from his window, was not for him, but for the young *fadais* who were willing to die in doing his will. A magnanimity hardly to be surpassed in this world. And he was a Spartan too, this Hasan. He slew both his sons for no apparent reason except that one of them was suspected of conniving at the murder of a *dai*, the other was seen drinking wine. And he himself—the ruthlessness of Logic, the irony of Fate!—

was slain by his own brother-in-law after a long and prosperous reign, and when old Omar was still rhyming in Neishapur.

Those who followed him also passed away in the popular fashion. Jelaluddin Hasan III poisoned his father because he could not wait to succeed him in the ordinary manner. Otherwise, he was a good man. He restored the old doctrine—secret principles for the initiated and Islam for the people—and no assassinations of interest occurred during his happy reign, except, of course, his own. Like his father, he, too, was quietly removed by poison. His son who succeeded him was an imbecile. He took the people into his confidence and revealed to them all the high mysteries of the Sect. Religion, he announced, is abolished forever: laws and moralities are extinct. The people applauded and gave themselves up to feasting and pleasure.

Nevertheless, this imbecile Sheikh ul-Jabal ruled for thirty years, and were it not for his son, he might have died a natural death. Ruknuddin who succeeded him was the last of the Assassin rulers in Persia and the most ambitious if not the most original. He sought the recognition of Europe: he dreamt of rising to respectability among kings. But the envoy he sent to the court of Henry III of England was not received with all the honors due to his rank. One of the King's bishops said something, in his presence, about Mohammedan pigs and hell-fire, which the envoy had to swallow and digest on his way back to his Master. Had Ruknuddin looked eastward, however, instead of westward for a sign, he might have saved himself the mortification of such European recognition.

For out of the heart of Asia at that time came forth the fierce Hulago—the British bishop must have blessed his soul—to bring the hell-fire and the pigs together. The Tartar hordes under his command, issuing from the fertile plains south of the Baikal Lake early in the thirteenth century, swept like a cyclone over Bokhara and Samarkand and Khorasan up to the

confines of Persia. One fortress after another fell before them, castle and palace
were razed to the dust, cities were sacked
and destroyed, and Alamut and Ruknuddin
were treated to a general massacre that
sent the shivers down the spine of Assas-
sindom. Thus the dynasty of Hasan ibn
Sabah was completely overthrown in
Persia.

But the Syrian branch, which was established during Hasan's time, was still beyond Hulago's power. It continued, even
after the fall of Ruknuddin and the capture
of Alamut, to be a red terror to rulers and
princes as well as to the Crusaders. The
reign of the dagger in Syria was based on
the principle of absolute impartiality. It
made no distinction between Mohammedans and Christians, Orientals and Euro-
peans. The followers of Bahram, the
Syrian Old Man of the Mountain, prac-
ticed the most unspeakable atrocities
against the inhabitants as well as against
those in power. Carrying off women and
children from the streets in open day, was

[43]

the least of their crimes. And they improved upon the method of their Persian colleagues by extending the privileges of their Sect to alien princes and rulers.

"They caused assassination to be committed," one historian states, "at the solicitation of other princes for motives of interest in which religion had no share." In other words, they were a corporation of professional murderers, whose services were at the disposal of any prince or ruler in trouble. It is this Syrian branch, which became independent of Alamut, that is known to the Crusaders. Count Raymond of Tripoli and Conrad of Montferrat were slain probably by the *fadais*, who had acquired so much power that every scoundrel assumed their name as a convenient cloak for his crimes. Their reign of terror struck he mightiest and the boldest with fear and trepidation. It produced two new diseases in the land—moral torpor and mental paralysis.

And the work of the dagger was reinforced with conspiracies and intrigues for additional power. Perhaps the Assassins wanted a window on the sea when they entered into a secret treaty with the Crusaders by which they were to barter Damascus for Tyre. But the plot was discovered in time, and the people of Damascus rose against them, massacring six thousand in the streets and crucifying the more prominent among them along the city walls. Aleppo and Diarbekr followed the example of Damascus. But these massacres had little or no effect, it seems, upon a Sect that lived by assassination. It continued to flourish, even after its power had been broken in Persia, until the Mamluk Sultan Bibars, a score of years later, set out from Egypt to imitate in Syria Hulago's example. And he was as successful as the Tartar chief. For the Assassins were ultimately out-assassinated, almost exterminated by Bibars, and their Sect was abolished,—"buried," as one historian puts it, "amidst the ruins of thrones and altars, and covered with the universal execration of mankind."

The fact is, however, that the remnants of it were driven into secrecy and silence; and some of them, till this day, are to be found in Kerman and Khorasan, where they are protected to some extent by British officials. And the Ismailites of upper Syria today, though they be suspected of nature-worship, have forgotten, through centuries of submission to the Turks, the use of the dagger,—they have lost the faculty of violence.

CHAPTER V

The Illuminati

Born of mysticism and religious chaos, the movements in the East against organized society were, nevertheless, concealed by the apostles of violence, under the cloak of religion. There have been similar movements in the West, which, under the mask of philosophy, sought to undermine all existing authority in the state and all creeds and moral codes in the nation.

Most prominent among these is the intellectual Bolshevism, which first appeared in Germany in the latter part of the 18th century. The rebel cry of a group of fanatics, who were then known as the Illuminati or Perfectibilists, is re-echoed today and translated into machine guns by the Sparticides, whose patron saint is not the Thracian gladiator and leader of the slaves against Rome in Pompei's time, but Adam Weishaupt, who adopted the name of

[47]

Spartacus. And the members of the secret society he founded assumed the names of Cato, Hannibal, Alcibiades and other heroes of antiquity.

Adam Weishaupt, who was Professor of Canon Law at the University of Ingolstadt, had studied with the Jesuits, was for a time a militant member of the Order and later became its bitterest enemy. When it was suppressed in Germany, Weishaupt proposed to found another order based upon the same principles of discipline, but with a vastly different object. His scheme was to establish a society which in time should govern the world by abolishing, as we shall see, Christianity and overturning all civil governments. He discussed with some of his Jesuit friends the more attractive, the innocuous features of his project, but they refused to have anything to do with it. Weishaupt then struck out alone, availing himself of the medium of his lecture room to spread among his pupils his pet theories of equality and internationalism, and his philosophy of the pastoral virtues. He drew for them fascinating pictures of a happy society, where "every office was held by a man of talent and virtue and every talent is set in a place fit for its exertion."

In the undercurrents of his Canon Law lectures, Weishaupt was a link between Rousseau and Hebert. Patriotism is a narrow-minded prejudice, incompatible with universal benevolence;—the princes and nobles—the diplomats of our day—instead of serving the people, served only their kings, and under the flattering idea of "the balance of power" they kept the nations in subjection;—the pernicious influence of accumulated property is an insurmountable obstacle to the happiness of any nation;—man has fallen from his high estate in civil society and only by returning to nature can he accomplish a complete regeneration. And now and then, not in the lectures perhaps, but certainly in the letters of Spartacus, he advocated the adoption of any means to an end. The preponderancy of good in the ultimate result consecrated every means, and wisdom and virtue consisted in properly determining the balance. Here we get his idea of Cosmopolitanism, or internationalism, which was to be promoted, when necessary, by violence.

Thus paving the way in his lecture room, which "became the seminary of Cosmopolitanism," he was able in 1776 to gather a few intellectual rebels, his staunch disciples, and form the secret society of the Perfectibilists, which later became known throughout Europe as the Illuminati. Its first object was to check the tyranny of princes and priests and establish a state of universal equality. It sought to enlist among its members Christians of every profession and especially free masons of the eclectic order, such as the Lodge Theodore of Good Council, which was founded in Munich in 1775 and became afterwards the principal centre of the Illuminati.

The members on admission were pledged to blind obedience to the order of their superiors. Their subservience was assured by a strict system of secret confessions and monthly reports checked by mutual espionage. And like the Jesuit Order, they made special efforts to enlist young men of wealth and rank and social importance, so that gradually, through them, they would control the mainsprings of all authority and power. Furthermore, like the secret societies of the East, its membership was divided into classes and degrees. But the free masons alone—a proof that it had abjured Christianity— were eligible to the degrees of regent and magnus, or masters of the higher mysteries.

All the members, however, were to be the beneficiaries of a system designed to free them from all religious prejudices, to cultivate among them the social virtues and to animate them by a great, a feasible and speedy prospect of universal happiness. (A sort of Get-Happy-Quick Scheme, indeed.) And this can only be realized in a state of liberty and moral and social equality, free from all the obstacles which subor-

dination, rank and riches throw in the way
of man. "Our secret association," wrote
Weishaupt, "works in a way that nothing
can withstand it, and man shall soon be
free and happy."

It worked, in fact, in many ways; one of
which was to unite and dominate through
the Lodge Theodore in Munich the various
secret societies of Europe. And more
secret ways, on which the higher mysteries
only can shed some light. For as far as the
public utterances of Weishaupt go, they
seem to embody nothing outside of a legit-
imate purpose to overturn the despotisms
of kings and priests and to free the mind
of man from political fallacies and religious superstitions. But when we penetrate
behind the veil, we find the dark currents
that connect the Illuminati with the Ismailites of Islam as well as with the Mazdakites of Persia.

All things, good and evil, come out, it
seems, of the East. The Illuminati, like
the Ismailites, dealt in allegories; and like
the Mazdakites, they played with fire. In

the letters of Spartacus-Weishaupt, if they are all authentic, is a complete revelation of the secret teachings and designs of the Order.

"The allegory on which I am to found the mysteries of the higher order," he writes to Cato (Zwack, a judge of Munich) "is the Fire-Worship of the Magi. We must have some worship,"—shades of the Old Man of the Mountain!—"and none is so apposite." And he goes on to give his own allegorical interpretation of Christianity. Jesus of Nazareth is made out to be "the Grand Master of the Order." For he taught the lesson of reason under the guise of religion; he combined his secret doctrines, which he revealed only to the chosen few, with the popular beliefs and customs of his time. Liberty and equality are the great aims of all his teachings; and these can only be attained through morality and virtue. Here is an example: Man has fallen from the condition of liberty and equality—the state of pure nature. He is under subordination and civil bondage, which are born of organized society. His submission is the Fall, the Original Sin. And the Kingdom of Grace is that of restoration by illumination, or through the *disciplina arcani* (secret disciplines) and the pastoral virtues. This is the New Birth.

All of which would seem quite innocuous, no better and no worse in fact than parlor anarchy or socialism. But the Illuminati did not stop here. They would restore man to his pristine purity, free him from all subjugation, raise him to his original state of liberty and equality, redeem him, in a word, and all mankind THROUGH SECRET SCHOOLS OF WISDOM. Here we get an intimation of the higher purpose, a peep into the higher mysteries, where even allegories are stripped of their seductive masks. But the teachings of the Assassins and the doctrines of the Ismailites are clothed, for the benefit of the Illuminati, in philosophic rags picked up at the doors of Spinoza and Plato. *All things are inherent in Nature* and *God and the*

World are one, may cover a few sore spots; but the nakedness here and there of Atheism, is as appalling as that of Hasan ibn Sabah, who denounced all religions as the contrivances of ambitious and wicked men. Immorality, too, suffers no disguise. And with these we are to have the Patriarchal State, based upon the Pastoral Virtues, where "the peasant, the citizen, and the householder" are sovereigns and where subordination and inequality are no more. They must vanish forever from the face of the earth.

"By this plan," writes Spartacus to Cato, "we shall direct all mankind. In this manner and by the simplest means we shall set all in motion and flames. The occupations must be so allotted and contrived that we may in secret influence all political transactions." And the list of the contents of a chest, which was discovered after the Order was suppressed by the Elector of Bavaria, gives us an idea of "the simplest means" of setting the world in flames, of destroying the universe in order to establish on its ruins the reign of the Pastoral Virtues.

Among the things mentioned in this list are explosives of various kinds, dynamite, "a composition which blinds and kills when spurted in the face," "a method for filling a bed-chamber with pestilential vapors," strange herbs for procuring abortion, and aphrodisiacs concealed in Latin names. Simpler by far is the method of the Assassins.

But unlike the Assassins and unlike his namesake, Spartacus and his followers were timid in action,—they lacked the heroic spark, and the self-sacrificing zeal. Their incendiarism was an abstraction. They only dreamed and philosophized. They had visions, too, of eternal bliss and voluptuous pleasures. For they were also to found a Lodge of Sister Illuminati. "It will be of great service," wrote Alcibiades, "and procure us both much information and money, and will suit charmingly the taste of many of our truest members who are lovers of the sex. It should consist of two classes, the virtuous and the free-hearted.''

But the members had some trouble, it seems, in achieving pristine purity and practicing the pastoral virtues. According to John Robison, who exposed the Order a few years after it was suppressed and who translated some of the letters of Spartacus, they were sneaky, white-livered rascals, without the virtue even of an Ismailite, who fought in the open or an Assassin, who sacrificed himself for a full share of Mohammed's paradise. Spartacus himself realized this and bemoaned it in print.

Thus, for instance, to Cato: ''Alcibiades sits the day long with the vintner's pretty wife and then sighs and pines. A few days ago at Corinth (they also gave modern cities ancient names), Tiberius attempted to ravish the wife of Democides, and her husband came in upon them. Good heavens, what Areopagitae I have got.''

Admitting that some of these Spartacus letters may be forgeries, designed to discredit the Order, there is nothing to disprove that among its secret practices the so-called *disciplina arcani* often became a bacchanalian orgy. For, all the pastoral and social virtues to the contrary, sensual pleasures were restored to the rank they hold in the Epicurean philosophy—but not openly proclaimed.

Herein they differ from the Bacchanalians of Rome, who, in the sixth century of the Republic, tried to cover with the wine-stained mantle of their god the most nefarious designs against the established authorities of the City and the State. But the Illuminati were secret worshippers of Bacchus, while they pretended to be votaries of Ceres. That they took the names of the heroes of antiquity in vain, is the least of their sins. And while secretly preparing their "pestilential vapors" and poison gases for the human race, formally and on stoical principles, they santioned only self-murder. They little realized, in doing this, that they were invoking in their justification the memory of Judas. Indeed, as far as they, at least, were concerned, Judas

THE DESCENT OF BOLSHEVISM

Iscariot was their patron saint. For as a
rule, rebels are loyal to each other, and
members of a secret society practice loy-
alty at least in self-defense. But the Illuminati spied upon, cheated and betrayed
each other.

Indeed, the downfall of the Order was
brought about by two of its own members
who, to save their own skin, revealed its
high mysteries to the authorities, before it
entered upon the tenth year of its "illumination." Whereupon the Bavarian Government issued an edict against it, many of its
members were deported, and Weishaupt
was deprived of his professorship and
banished to Switzerland. Its secret doctrines, however, continued to spread over
Europe. They leavened more or less all
the subsequent revolutions and found good
soil for a time in the United States.

John Humphrey Noyes, who became,
through what he called "a second conver-
sion," a perfectionist, founded the Oneida
Community and, harking back to the Illuminati and beyond them towards the East

[59]

to the Mazdakites, tried to establish a utopia, in which all things were held in common. For Noyes and his followers, who accepted the reign of God, there was no longer any law or rule of duty. They were a law unto themselves. They were free to do as they pleased. And under the influence of the divine Spirit, which dwelt in them, they could do only what was right. They were perfect—Perfectionists. And they were equalitarians: they held all things in common. And they gave up all religious observances, like the Ismailites, renounced allegiance to the United States Government, and instituted, what was called, "a complex system of marriage." But complex or simple, John Noyes could not by any marriage system or lack of it, raise communism to a virtue or an acceptable legal formula, or even screen it under the semblance of religion. Noyes was a mild and sincere fanatic. But his Community, after a checkered career of forty years, developed into—and is still to-day—a fruit canning establishment—

The Oneida Company, Ltd.! But he was not responsible for this vulgar metamorphosis of his Utopia; for long before that, when his marriage system was exposed, he fled with a few of his followers to Canada.

Many other experiments in universal brotherhood and equality took place in the United States, and were conducted in a peaceful and truly philosophic or religious manner. In spite of which, their success was only temporary. Human nature itself was against them—did not respect even the undoubted sincerity of their founders. I need but mention two other utopians in proof of this. There was Thomas Lake Harris, who established the Brotherhood of the New Life and who, having survived it and its internal dissensions, set to work finally as a vinyardist in Santa Rosa, California. And there was the French reformer, Etienne Cabet, who fled his own country and sought to establish, in 1848, the reign of equality and brotherhood in Texas. But the internal dissensions of his Icarian Community and the external suspicions that darkened its horizon, marred, alas, the happiness of its followers, and ultimately placed on its door the seal of bankruptcy and failure.

CPSIA information can be obtained at www.ICGtesting.com
Printed in the USA
240493LV00017B/129/P